MW00944761

How to Talk to God
Developing a Meaningful Practice of Prayer

RYAN BENNETT

Copyright © 2017 by Ryan Bennett

All rights reserved. No part of this publication may be
reproduced, distributed, or transmitted in any form or by any
means, including photocopying, recording, or other electronic or
mechanical methods, without the prior written permission of the
author, except in the case of brief quotations embodied in
critical reviews and certain other noncommercial
uses permitted by copyright law.

Unless otherwise indicated, all Scripture quotations are taken
from the Holy Bible, New International Version (NIV)
copyright © 1973, 1978, 1984, 2011.

CONTENTS

CHAPTER 1

Barriers to Prayer

———————

Prayer is supposed to be a rich and meaningful conversation with God. It should be what anchors us, what connects us to Heaven itself as we take every need great and small to the God of the universe. It can be our joy, our solace, and our strength when the world around us seems to be crumbling. Prayer should, could, and is supposed to be all of these things but often it isn't. Speaking for myself, ever since I became a follower of Jesus, I wanted that kind of prayer life: The kind of prayer life that was vital, that was real, that made a difference in my life and the lives of people around me. However, for a long time prayer felt too intangible, too lofty, and honestly too hard. If you are a Christian, and perhaps even if you aren't, you know that prayer is important. We're exhorted to pray in sermons, and the Bible is full of people praying and pouring out their hearts to God. We know we should be praying more and more deeply, but often our experience of prayer seems weak and shallow.

I think for most of us prayer is kind of like exercise. We know we need it. We know it's good for us. We may even dabble in it from time to time, but we just can't seem to make the habit stick, and we don't often see the results we want. We're either too busy or we feel like we don't know how. I think the comparison can be taken even farther, because prayer helps us build our faith. It works our spiritual muscles in a way that nothing else does. Yes, we need to be reading the Bible, we need to be in community with other Christians, and we need to be doing a whole host of other things to maintain our spiritual health, but prayer is an activity that is at the core of our faith. It connects us intimately with God in a way that brings life to all of our other activities. To borrow from the Apostle Paul, if we read the Bible all day long and can quote Scripture in every occasion but we don't pray, what power can our words have? If we faithfully attend church and spend time with other Christians, but we don't pray, what strength does our love have? If we obey Jesus at every point but skip prayer, have we really even understood his teaching in the first place?

We could give a lot of reasons for why we don't pray or why our practice of prayer isn't what we would like it to be, but essentially they are all versions of the same two problems.

1. We don't have time.
   - *or* -
2. We don't really know how to pray.

Not enough time or too busy

First, let's talk about busyness. We are all busy. Life is hectic and sometimes it seems like we can't even find a few minutes to ourselves each day. How can we make time for prayer when it seems like there is always too much to do and not enough time to do it? Just like with exercise, who has the time? Maybe your schedule is so full that you can't spare a minute, if that's the case I can't help you except to say that you should probably relax a little, but *having* time to pray is about *making* time to pray. If you don't *make time*, you'll never *have time*. This all comes down to priorities. You'll make time for the things you value and if prayer is a value and you make it a priority, you'll always be able to make time for it. Plus, once you start to see the benefits, just like with exercise, you'll be motivated to keep going. In this book we'll look at some very simple and practical ways to make time for prayer, so that you'll always have time to pray.

How should I pray?

Second, how should we pray? If you are anything like me, even if you set aside time to pray and put yourself in an environment where you aren't going to be interrupted, you somehow still manage to get distracted. You start praying, your mind starts to wander, and before you know it you've entirely forgotten what you were doing. Then, again if you're like me, you get frustrated and think, "Ok, focus, pray!" Then within a minute you're distracted again and the whole process feels more discouraging than encouraging, more like a defeat than a victory. It's ok. It takes practice. We have to train ourselves to pray, and we have to be taught how to pray. If it were that easy and natural, then we wouldn't need to be told to do it. But there are better and worse ways to pray. There are methods and patterns that can help keep us focused and push through towards moments of sublime intimacy with God. In this book we'll explore some of these methods, so that you'll never be at a loss again for how you should pray.

Conclusion

Have hope. You, despite busyness, can make time for prayer. It's possible. I want to help you carve out time for meeting with the God of the universe, and the more you do so, the more you'll want to pray, and the sweeter it will become. You can also learn how to pray in ways that are meaningful, powerful and biblical. The book of James in the New Testament says, "The prayer of a righteous person is powerful and effective. Elijah was a human being, even as we are. He prayed earnestly that it would not rain, and it did not rain on the land for three and a half years. Again, he prayed, and the heavens gave rain, and the earth produced its crops" (Jas 16b–18). We can have effective prayer lives. But we need a model, someone who made time for prayer even in the midst of busyness and someone who can teach us how to pray. We need a model, but more than that we need someone who can come alongside us in prayer, lift us up, and intercede for us. We need Jesus, and it is to his prayer life that we now turn.

CHAPTER 2

Jesus: Our Model in Prayer

Jesus in the Gospels

We can find no better teacher in the practice of prayer than Jesus himself. The Gospels are full of references to Jesus' prayer life, how he taught his disciples to pray and they are filled with encouragements from Jesus *to pray*. Jesus truly practiced what he preached and while we could turn to any Gospel and learn a great deal about prayer from him, the Gospel of Luke bursts with Jesus' prayer life.

Luke himself seems particularly interested in highlighting prayer both in Jesus' life and in the life of the early church. He mentions prayer over twenty times in his Gospel and then mentions it again over thirty times in the book of Acts. Luke seems at pains to emphasize that the mission and work of God moves forward especially through prayer. But what does Luke teach us about how Jesus prayed?

One thing we learn is that Jesus went out of his way to make time and space for prayer. Luke says, "But Jesus often withdrew to lonely places and prayed" (Lk 5:13). This was in the context of Jesus' ministry gaining notoriety and success. After some of his initial healings, crowds were seeking him out. Many were probably looking to be healed themselves. Others were probably curious to see a miracle or to see if what was being said about him was true. At any rate, Jesus had no shortage of work to do and no shortage of demand on his time. Yet Luke makes a point of stating that Jesus *often* got away by himself in order to pray. This was a regular practice that Jesus had, setting apart time just to be by himself with the Father. No situation was too urgent, no crisis so important that Jesus couldn't put prayer before all else. In fact, for Jesus it was just the opposite; *prayer* was so urgent, *prayer* was so important that everything else had to wait.

His daily life and ministry demanded frequent times apart for prayer, and large decisions and important moments needed prayer that much more. Before selecting the twelve apostles Luke says, "One of those days Jesus went out to a mountainside to pray, and spent the night praying to God" (Lk 6:12). Picking the twelve was an important undertaking. There would be others involved in Jesus' mission, he picks 70 later on in the Gospel, but these twelve are leaders and pillars, they are foundational members of his movement with special access to Jesus himself. Before Jesus made such an important step, he thought it was necessary to get away and spend the whole night in prayer. The same thing happens before his arrest and crucifixion.

> Jesus went out as usual to the Mount of Olives, and his disciples followed him. On reaching the place, he said to them, "Pray that you will not fall into temptation." He withdrew about a stone's throw

beyond them, knelt down and prayed, "Father, if you are willing, take this cup from me; yet not my will, but yours be done." An angel from heaven appeared to him and strengthened him. And being in anguish, he prayed more earnestly, and his sweat was like drops of blood falling to the ground (Lk 22:39–44).

In key moments in Jesus' ministry he is always praying. The cross was the climax of his ministry and the culmination for which he came and there, before that crucial moment, he prays with even greater intensity. Jesus knew that prayer was the key to accomplishing his task. A point he tried to make moments later to his disciples. Luke says, "When he rose from prayer and went back to the disciples, he found them asleep, exhausted from sorrow. 'Why are you sleeping?' he asked them. 'Get up and pray so that you will not fall into temptation'" (Lk 22:45–46). He attempted to warn his disciples in that very moment that they would face a similar trial and that they should pray so they would be ready, but as was often the case, they failed. They were always slow to learn some of his most important lessons.

Luke talks about other times where Jesus and his disciples were "praying in private" (Lk 9:18). Jesus modeled his prayer life before his followers. He was teaching them, and us as well, that private, separated, intentional prayer was at the core of what it means to be his follower. Prayer is where power comes from. Prayer is where wisdom comes from. Prayer is where victory comes from. Jesus invited his disciples into his intimacy with the Father so that they could carry his mission forward, and it eventually rubbed off. The book of Acts is a testament to the fact that Jesus' way of prayer finally hit home with his disciples and the results were uncontainable. In chapter one the disciples are praying constantly together until the Holy Spirit comes to empower them and send them out in power to preach the

Gospel. In chapter two the early church devotes itself to "the apostles' teaching and to fellowship, to the breaking of bread and to prayer" (Acts 2:42). The next chapter shows Peter and John going to the temple at one of the set times of prayer. In chapter four, after the arrest and release of Peter and John, the disciples join together to pray that God would do wonders, work miracles and make Jesus known and "after they prayed, the place where they were meeting was shaken. And they were all filled with the Holy Spirit and spoke the word of God boldly" (Acts 4:31). In chapter six the twelve apostles decide that their chief occupation must be giving themselves to the word of God and prayer (6:4). They had enough evidence that prayer worked, and now they realized what Jesus had always tried to teach them. Prayer is at the heart of God's work because prayer takes us to the heart of God. When you and I grasp this we'll never be able to make another excuse not to pray. We won't be stopped from praying. Once we glimpse what Jesus taught, what his disciples finally understood that prayer is the key that unlocks the floodgates of heaven, we'll only wonder why we don't use it more.

Our High Priest who even now intercedes for us

Jesus didn't just model prayer for his disciples during his lifetime; he also made some pretty amazing promises about prayer to his disciples for after his death. In John chapter 14 Jesus says,

> Very truly I tell you, whoever believes in me will do the works I have been doing, and they will do even greater things than these, because I am going to the Father. And I will do whatever you ask in my name, so that the Father may be glorified in the Son. You may ask me for anything in my name, and I will do it. If you love me, keep my commands. And I will ask

the Father, and he will give you another advocate to help you and be with you forever—the Spirit of truth. The world cannot accept him, because it neither sees him nor knows him. But you know him, for he lives with you and will be in you. I will not leave you as orphans; I will come to you. Before long, the world will not see me anymore, but you will see me. Because I live, you also will live. On that day you will realize that I am in my Father, and you are in me, and I am in you. Whoever has my commands and keeps them is the one who loves me. The one who loves me will be loved by my Father, and I too will love them and show myself to them (Jn 14:12–21).

Jesus promised that those who follow him would do greater works than he did because after Jesus' returns to the Father, the Spirit would come to empower his disciples for mission. This empowering for mission is also an empowering to pray. Paul seems to be almost paraphrasing and expanding Jesus' words in Romans chapter 8 when he says,

For those who are led by the Spirit of God are the children of God. The Spirit you received does not make you slaves, so that you live in fear again; rather, the Spirit you received brought about your adoption to sonship. And by him we cry, "*Abba*, Father." The Spirit himself testifies with our spirit that we are God's children. Now if we are children, then we are heirs—heirs of God and co-heirs with Christ, if indeed we share in his sufferings in order that we may also share in his glory…. In the same way, the Spirit helps us in our weakness. We do not know what we ought to pray for, but the Spirit himself intercedes for us through wordless groans. And he who searches our hearts knows the mind of the Spirit, because the Spirit intercedes for God's people in accordance with the will of God (Rom 8:14–17, 26–27).

Jesus and Paul make the promise that the Spirit, who marks us as children of God, helps us to pray. He helps us to pray as we should. The disciples after Pentecost didn't just pray more, but they prayed with more power because the Spirit of God was in them helping them to pray.

We stand in a better position to pray after Jesus' death and resurrection, because we are not alone when we pray, we have the very Spirit of God *in us* praying together with us. What specific advantages does having the Spirit give? First, the Spirit gives us assurance that we belong to God. We're not orphans, not outsiders, not strangers, but God's own children coming before him with our requests. We stand in the same position as Jesus, which is that we are heirs of God. We're children of the Father with all the intimacy, affection, and care that our loving heavenly Father can give, but even more than that our Father is lord and master of all there is. He has every resource at his disposal, and everything we ask for is in his power to give. Our Father isn't stingy but is generous to the point of excess. He gives rain to the unjust, takes care of sparrows, and makes the flowers of the field more beautifully adorned than king Solomon. We have this access because we have the Spirit. Second, the Spirit himself intercedes for us in our prayers. The Spirit stands like a translator between us and God making the intentions of our prayer come through despite our weakness and inadequacy. In a way this makes it impossible to pray wrongly. Every prayer offered in faith by the power of the Spirit is heard and answered, because it is transformed into a prayer that is in accordance with the will of God. Perhaps an example would help, we can agree that if anyone prayed by the Spirit at all times it was Jesus. Jesus received the answers to everything that he prayed for, but right before his crucifixion in the Garden of Gethsemane, he asked that he would be spared the ordeal he was about to face. He knew the pain, the shame, and the separation from the Father that was awaiting him and he asked for another way, but he prayed that ultimately God's will would be done. Jesus knew God's will, but the Spirit brought the will of God to bear through Jesus' prayer. Jesus asked for options knowing his prayer couldn't fail, because the Spirit would intercede and grant it according to the will of God. We can pray in the same way knowing the Spirit will use even our weakest prayers to bring about what God wants. The Spirit knows God and knows us better than we know ourselves; therefore he perfectly presents our true needs to God and perfectly receives for us what God desires to give. This should give us great confidence in prayer, because ultimately we can't fail! The only failure is not to pray.

Don't wait any longer to start praying, because you feel like you don't know how. Start now knowing if you belong to Christ you have his Spirit inside you standing ready to pray with you and making your prayers heard. Of course, there are better and worse ways to pray, and we'll look at them soon, but start putting prayer into practice now trusting the Spirit to lead you, guide you, and intercede for you. In the next chapter we'll look at how to make prayer a habit and practice so central in your life that you'll never want to give it up.

CHAPTER 3

Putting Prayer into Practice:
How to make time for prayer

───────────────

Now it becomes real. This is where we move from the realm of encouragement to pray to prayer being an actual practice in your life. If prayer is anything, it is an action. It is something we do, not just something we think about. Having more understanding of prayer is no substitute for prayer itself. Knowledge matters, but practice matters more. Just like knowing what you should eat matters, but actually eating well matters a lot more.

Carving out time

Martin Luther famously said, "I have so much to do today that I'm going to need to spend three hours in prayer in order to be able to get it all done."

If we had this attitude toward prayer, that prayer was how we accomplished the work of a busy day instead of something that distracts us from our work, we wouldn't need an encouragement to make time for prayer. I'm convinced we can get there. We can get to a place where we see prayer as so vital and necessary that we couldn't imagine trying to get by with less but would instead plot how we can get more. While three hours in prayer may not be possible or necessary for all of us, with wisdom and intentionality we can all carve out more time for prayer.

How?

Having the proper attitude and desire is the first step, which hopefully you do, but we can't get to a place of praying at all times and in all occasions until we pray at some times and on some occasions. In attempting to create a regular practice of prayer it might help to answer the following questions. When should you pray? Where should you pray? How can you make time for prayer? How much should you pray?

First, *when* should you pray? This is an easier question to answer than how much to pray because there are some biblical patterns. One pattern is praying three times a day. The best example of this is Daniel. In the book of Daniel, the royal officials of King Darius are jealous of Daniel and try to find a way to discredit him. The only way they can think to do so is to use his devotion to God against him. They convince the king to make a decree that throughout the kingdom for thirty days everyone should pray to Darius and anyone who prays to another god will be punished by being thrown into a den of lions. At this point the text says, "Now when Daniel learned that the decree had been published, he went home to his upstairs room where the windows opened toward Jerusalem. Three times a day he got down on his knees and prayed, giving thanks to his God, just as he had done before" (Dan 6:10). The story ends with Daniel being thrown into the lions' den, but he is protected from the lions by an angel and ultimately those who were jealous of him suffer the fate they had planned for Daniel. The book of Acts also suggests that the apostles followed this same practice of praying saying that Peter and John went to the temple at three in the afternoon for prayer. It is a practice of recognizing morning, noon, and night that we are dependent on God. Just like we survive on three meals a day, we live by three times of prayer a day.

The Psalms, which could be considered the Bible's prayer book, present a pattern of morning and evening prayer. In Judaism, a day is marked from sunset to sunset instead of from sunrise to sunrise. A new day starts at sundown, which shows up in Psalm 4 and 5. Psalm 4 says, "Tremble and do not sin; when you are on your beds, search your hearts and be silent. Offer the sacrifices of the righteous and trust in the Lord…. In peace I will lie down and sleep, for you alone, Lord, make me dwell in safety" (Ps 4:4–5,8). Then Psalm 5 says, "In the morning, Lord, you hear my voice; in the morning I lay my requests before you and wait expectantly" (Ps 5:3). In the morning we ask God for what we need for that day, then wait to see what he provides, while the evening is the time to reflect and confess our sin to God trusting in him to protect us through the night. These two Psalms present prayer as the bookends of our day, starting and ending each day with prayer. Our life is lived between these times; reminding us that God is the beginning and the end, the alpha and the omega.

Both in the story of Daniel and in the Psalms, prayer starts and ends the day. Daniel simply has one more time for prayer in the middle of the day. I haven't always prayed in the middle of the day, but during times when I have, I've found it helps bring me back to God in the midst of my busyness. In one job I had I would often take a walk during my lunch break and pray. I would eat as quickly as I could and go outside to walk and pray. It was only ever a 15 or 20-minute walk, but I would take the concerns that had built up over the day to God and ask for help to do my work in a way that would honor him. I always came back more full of peace and better able to love my coworkers. So, if you can do it, try it and see what happens. Even if you can only get five minutes alone to stop and pray, it would be worth it. The important thing to remember, though, with set times of prayer is that there is no command to follow a certain pattern. These fixed times are to help us, not God. A rhythm of prayer keeps us centered and focused on our heavenly Father, but he is always there waiting to hear and respond whenever we come. It is for our benefit that we have a regular pattern of coming to him. He is gracious and good enough to receive us anytime. That being said, however, it seems psychologically significant that we should begin and end our days in prayer. If you can, try, even if just as an experiment for a while to see what difference it makes. If you're having trouble making time, we'll come back to that shortly. My practice is to try to spend a significant portion of time praying in the morning, then to pray together with my wife at night before bed. It gives a rhythm and balance to my spiritual life that informs and shapes everything else.

One theme that we see in Daniel, as well as Jesus' teaching on prayer in Matthew 6, is that having a consistent *place* of prayer matters. Daniel prays in front of his window opened toward Jerusalem and Jesus says, "But when you pray, go into your room, close the door and pray to your Father, who is unseen. Then your Father, who sees what is done in secret, will reward you" (Mt 6:6). So, where should you pray? The easy answer is anywhere that makes it easier to pray. Where can you be the most alone, the freest from distraction, and the most at ease to commune with God? You might have to get up earlier to have this peace and quiet. Perhaps you can pray in your car on your way to work. Wherever it is, make a habit of praying there limiting distractions as much as you can. Put your phone on silent, or better, don't even bring it with you to your prayer place. Moses was told to take off his sandals when he approached the burning bush because he was standing on holy ground. Let us approach our places of prayer in the same way expecting God to show up. One reason it is so hard for us to hear him is because we don't have enough silence built into our lives to listen. That simple act of cutting the cord, even for a short time, will go a long way to make our place of prayer a calm and sacred space preparing us to hear from our heavenly Father.

If you can get out into nature, do so. I live in the city, and I love it, but every time I get out and glimpse hills, trees, and fields something in me wakes up and comes alive. Even if it is just a nearby park, some secluded green space, or your own backyard, praying there can give you a chance to appreciate the God who spoke the universe into existence and hung the stars in the sky. The Pilgrims called nature one of God's two books about himself, the other being Scripture itself. Being in God's creation can help us praise him because we're confronted with his creative power and beauty. We often see people in Scripture going up on mountains to pray. Abraham, Moses, and Jesus are prime examples of people going up a mountain to meet with God. One aspect of having to go up a mountain for prayer is physically leaving the hustle and bustle of the world below and literally getting a different view of it. The things that seemed so big, so intimidating and so pressing look small and insignificant from the top of a mountain. They lose some of their power over us and we're more open for God to intervene. Not many have this option, but it goes to show that our physical location has a psychological effect upon us. Make your habitual place of prayer your mountaintop where you are prepared for God to come and speak to you.

How can you make time for prayer? This is often our greatest challenge, and I want to offer some very practical answers. But it bears repeating that if we don't see the infinite value of prayer, we'll never make time for it. Hopefully the earlier part of this book convinced you of some of that value. If not, there is an appendix of books at the end of this book that will convince you beyond a doubt that prayer matters, and if your heart is cold toward prayer, spend time with these masters and it will be set on fire for prayer.

However, my first council for how to value and make time for prayer is pray for it. Instead of trying to work up the desire yourself, ask God for it. If you pray for 30 seconds once a week, make part of that prayer the simple request that God would give you a desire to pray more. If there is one prayer you can expect will be granted, it is this one. Nothing could be more according to the will of God than you spending more time face to face with your heavenly Father, and God is gracious enough and good enough to give you what you're asking for. Imagine a child coming to his father and saying, "Dad I love you, but I don't know how to spend time with you. Could you help me?" What father's heart wouldn't break and do everything in his power to make this request a reality, and we can trust our heavenly Father that much more to answer this kind of prayer. So, if you're struggling, start here. Start with the good news that God loves you so much that he sent his son to cross heaven and earth to die for you, and he will do everything in his power to bring you to himself. Pray for the desire to pray, and it will come.

If you have the desire, but the time is still hard to come by, the simplest solution is to wake up earlier or stay up later to pray. Personally, I prefer to wake up earlier to pray because I feel like it helps me start the day in a better posture. By the end of the day normally I just want to rest and relax, so forgetting to pray becomes easier. However, this is just a personal preference. If making time for prayer is easier for you in the evening, then, by all means, pray at night. If, though, you decide that you want to get up earlier to pray, here are a few simple ways to make it happen. First, you need to go to bed at a reasonable time or go to bed earlier than you have been, even a few minutes can make a big difference in helping you feel more awake when you get up. Second, add time gradually. Don't try to go from getting up at 7am every day to getting up at 6am. Perhaps you have tremendous will power and can simply make yourself do it, but I know that I would fail and my failure would discourage me. What I have done before is get up five minutes earlier every week until I was able to get up to the amount of time I wanted to pray. It may not sound like much, but each month you can add twenty minutes to your time of prayer and relatively quickly carve out a significant amount of time to commune with God. Third, if you're going to try to get up earlier for prayer, do something to help you wake up. Have coffee, take a shower, exercise or go for a quick walk outside. Just do something quick to wake up. It's embarrassing the number of times I have fallen asleep praying in the morning, particularly if I'm trying to be quiet and keep the lights low to not disturb anyone else in the house. If you wake up fresh every morning, count yourself blessed, but for everyone else, do whatever works to get you up and keep you up.

Adding time for prayer in the morning or the evening is the easiest and most natural way to build the habit of persistent communion with God. If you are wondering if this will take away time from the other things you need to do, rest assured it won't, and you can do a little experiment to prove it to yourself. Try keeping a "time journal" for yourself for one week. What is a time journal? People attempting to lose weight have often done so very successfully using a "food journal", which means for a period of time they write down everything they eat in a notebook. Most of the time when you're overeating you aren't aware of it. You think you just had cereal for breakfast, leftovers for lunch, and spaghetti for dinner and that's it. However, you forget that you had a muffin and orange juice later in the morning, then someone brought in cake for a birthday and you had a piece, finally you had several cookies as a late snack right before you went to bed. If you're forced to write down everything you eat, you get a better picture of where all your calories are coming from, and because you have to write it down, it becomes a mental check for whether you should actually eat it or not. A time journal is the same thing but for how you use your time. Take a notebook and simply record everything you do during the day. When I tried this, my journal was just a series of bullet points that looked like this:

- Woke up – 7am
- Shower – 7:05am
- Breakfast – 7:30am
- Etc.

I wrote down everything I was doing at a given time, but I also had to write down when I was wasting time. If you get on Facebook, write it down. If you start watching videos on Youtube, write it down. It only took me a few days, to realize that I was mindlessly surfing the internet an average of an hour and a half every day. Just knowing that helped me break the habit and cut down on wasting time. If you feel like you never have time, try keeping a time journal for just a week and you'll realize you are probably wasting way more time than you think. We all get the same amount of time every day. It is up to us to decide what we do with it. Would you rather scroll Facebook for hours on end looking at pictures of your middle school friend's cousin's wedding or develop the kind of relationship with God in prayer that brings life, joy, peace, and power? I'm not saying that these things are sin or that you should never get on the internet again, but for most of us we say that we wish we could pray but we don't have time, however, we give the time we do have to such meaningless things when we could have so much more. C.S. Lewis said that we are like children making mud pies in the slums, when we could have a vacation at the beach. We're satisfied with too little when God is offering us our heart's desires if we would only come to him.

We have talked about when to pray, where to pray, and how to make time for prayer, but we still haven't talked about how much we should pray. So, how much should you pray? The simple answer is… more. Paul tells us that we should, "Rejoice always, pray continually, give thanks in all circumstances; for this is God's will for you in Christ Jesus" (1 Thess 5:16–18). He also tells the Ephesians, "[P]ray in the Spirit on all occasions with all kinds of prayers and requests. With this in mind, be alert and always keep on praying for all the Lord's people" (Eph 6:18). Paul's command is to pray as much as possible and then some. As I said earlier, in order to learn to pray at all times in all places, it is best to start with praying at some times and in some places. Without a consistent practice of a fixed time for prayer, it is incredibly difficult to learn to pray without ceasing. Perhaps some can, but I know I cannot. For me personally, I've found that a fixed time of prayer of one hour was what made the difference in my prayer life. Before I decided that I wanted to build up to an hour of prayer a day, I was only praying an average of ten minutes a day and that was just ten minutes of trying to pray. I would start to pray, my mind would wander, then I would remember I was supposed to be praying, try again, and just repeat the pattern the whole time until I would finally stop ashamed and defeated. I slowly added five minutes a week to my time of prayer and once I was over

45 minutes the whole process took on a different aspect. I stopped trying to pray and started praying. Before I was always racking my brain to think of things to pray for, but then so many things started to come to my mind that I could pray for that I realized I would have to pray about them later on in the day. This was my practice right up until we had a child, then it was thrown into disarray for quite some time, but knowing that it worked once I used the same process of adding up time for prayer little by little until I got back to my goal.

At different stages of life different responsibilities will occupy you, so I can't tell you what number you should aim for when it comes to set times of prayer. However, I would say don't try to get away with the least amount that you can do. That's thinking about it from the wrong direction, thinking that prayer takes away time from what you need to do instead of helping you do it. Just to drive the point home, let's look at the quote we started with from Martin Luther, "I have so much to do today that I'm going to need to spend three hours in prayer in order to be able to get it all done." It is often said that prayer moves the hand that moves the world, and if that is the case we'll see more results the more we ask God to do.

Praying without ceasing

We have been talking about making a set time for prayer, which is fundamental to developing our prayer lives, but the Bible goes beyond that when it talks about prayer. As we just saw, Paul encourages us to pray continually and on all occasions with all kinds of prayers, and the history of the church is full of people who have become spiritual giants because they took Scripture at its word. But how do we get there? If you have developed a consistent and rich fixed time of prayer, the next step is to let that slowly bleed over into praying while you're doing other activities. My advice would be to start with more "mindless" activities that don't take much mental energy to do but could be good occasions to pray. A few examples come to mind. Praying while cleaning or doing the dishes is a perfect way to start. Your mind is normally wandering during these activities anyway, so why not attempt to turn these moments into times of prayer? If you drive, your commute to work can be a great time to have a conversation with God. During college I had a part time job as a cashier. A lot of my time was spent standing waiting for people to come to my line and check out of the store. I decided to try to fill my time standing and waiting for costumers with prayer, which not only gave me way more time to be in God's presence but it had an interesting side effect. I was infinitely more patient, compassionate, and helpful to the people I was serving. In my mind I would pray for them as they were in my line, which made me more eager to talk to them, and more eager to hear what they had to say. Often, we would get into very natural spiritual conversations without me trying because God was present in a very real way. A lot of jobs are much more mentally demanding than the one I had, but my point is simply to try to fill those dead moments, those moments when you must be physically present but when you let your mind go elsewhere, turn those moments into times of pray. Throughout the history of the church monks have given themselves to a life of prayer and physical work and often monasteries would have a sign hanging over each side of the door as the monks entered and exited. The sign over the door going in said "Prayer is work" and the sign over the door as they went out said, "Work is prayer." If we remember that, that it takes work to pray and that our work in the world should be infused with prayer, then it won't be too long before we find ourselves praying continually and in every situation.

Experiencing results

So far, we've just been looking at building prayer into a habit, which is often the first and most important step, but the reason we pray isn't simply to have a habit of praying, to feel good about how much we are praying, rather it is to pour out our hearts to God and see him answer. I think prayer in many respects is similar to exercise. Normally we start exercising because we want to lose weight and get in shape. Once we start seeing some progress it gives us motivation to keep going and perhaps even to increase our efforts. Over time you actually start to enjoy the process and while results still matter, the very act of exercising becomes enjoyable, and once that happens it becomes harder to break the habit than to keep it. Prayer works in a similar way. If you don't have a consistent practice of prayer at first it can be hard to build, but once you start to experience the benefits you'll be encouraged to pray that much more, and over time the combination of the answers that you see and the joy that spending time with the God who loves you more than you can possibly comprehend brings, you won't be able to stop praying.

But how do you see results in prayer? I, probably like you, have prayed for many things that didn't happen. I've prayed for jobs that I didn't get, healing for people who didn't get better, and a whole host of things that I didn't get clear answers to. Did I not have enough faith, maybe, but in most cases I don't think that is the reason we don't receive what we ask for. We'll come back to the subject of unanswered prayer later, but before then we can say a few things about experiencing results. First, God is not our genie. His purpose isn't to grant our wishes and desires as if he is the slave and we are the masters. It is quite the reverse, and the fact that he even condescends to hear and answer our personal prayers is astounding. No, God is the master and we are servants demanding resources from him to carry out his will. Another reason we don't receive what we want is our motivation for asking. In the book of James, he says, "When you ask, you do not receive, because you ask with wrong motives, that you may spend what you get on your pleasures" (Jas 4:3). James says when our purpose is simply to get what we want so that we can enjoy ourselves, then we miss prayer's true purpose and it's no surprise that God doesn't give it to us.

If we ask and we don't receive, we need to look at our own hearts and examine what our motivation is for asking. Jesus gives some amazing promises about what God will do for us through prayer, with the condition that we ask it in his name. This doesn't mean that saying "in Jesus' name" at the end of every prayer is the secret to being heard. It's not a magic formula for getting whatever we want. The way to understand asking for something in Jesus' name is to remember that a name represents a person. In the Old Testament, God was deeply concerned about the status of his name, which carried with it his reputation. If God's people acted in a way that dishonored his name, they dishonored him before the world and made people think less of Israel's God. However, when his name was honored, then his reputation is upheld and he is seen for being as glorious, powerful, and majestic as he is. When we pray in Jesus' name, we're praying that Jesus would be upheld, uplifted, and made known for being as wonderful as he is. Answered prayers are signs pointing to his goodness and power. Jesus said in John, "Very truly I tell you, whoever believes in me will do the works I have been doing, and they will do even greater things than these, because I am going to the Father. **And I will do whatever you ask in my name, so that the Father may be glorified in the Son.** You may ask me for anything in my name, and I will do it" (Jn 14:12–14). The key phrase is "so that the Father may be glorified." If answers to prayer bring glory to God, those are the kinds of prayers that

Jesus answers.

We're moving deeper into real prayer at this point. Where we are truly seeking to please God and glorify God through what we are praying. Everything said before still holds true. We have the Spirit interceding for us. We have a gracious and powerful heavenly Father ready to hear us, but if we are to grow in prayer and grow in our effectiveness in praying then we need to learn how to pray according to God's will. Rest assured that this doesn't mean knowing God's secret plan for everything, but rather it's about praying according to what God has already made abundantly clear in his Word. Scripture teaches us to pray according to God's will, so that we know how to ask God to answer the kind of prayer that he said that he would answer. So, let's turn to one of the most famous prayers of all time to learn how Jesus taught his followers to pray according to the will of God.

CHAPTER 4

"This is how you should pray…": The Lord's Prayer

Earlier we looked at Jesus' own prayer life, and saw that prayer was crucial to his ministry. He was often getting away to be alone in prayer. His disciples following him would have learned firsthand the importance he placed on prayer through his actions, but he goes farther and draws back the curtain on what is taking place between him and his Father. Jesus taught his disciples a way of praying that if we are at all serious about growing our prayer lives, we need to spend some time learning from it.

The Lord's Prayer

In Matthew chapter six Jesus teaches on how his followers are to carry out their acts of devotion to God. He teaches them about giving, praying and fasting. The truth that underlies all three is that they are to be done solely and simply for God and not for human recognition, because

God sees what is done in secret, we can trust him to reward us for the things we do for him. Sandwiched between giving and fasting, Jesus presents his teaching on prayer. He says,

> And when you pray, do not be like the hypocrites, for they love to pray standing in the synagogues and on the street corners to be seen by others. Truly I tell you, they have received their reward in full. But when you pray, go into your room, close the door and pray to your Father, who is unseen. Then your Father, who sees what is done in secret, will reward you. And when you pray, do not keep on babbling like pagans, for they think they will be heard because of their many words. Do not be like them, for your Father knows what you need before you ask him.

> This, then, is how you should pray:

> "Our Father in heaven,
> hallowed be your name,
> your kingdom come,
> your will be done,
> on earth as it is in heaven.
> Give us today our daily bread.
> And forgive us our debts,
> as we also have forgiven our debtors.
> And lead us not into temptation,
> but deliver us from the evil one."

> For if you forgive other people when they sin against you, your heavenly Father will also forgive you. But if you do not forgive others their sins, your Father will not forgive your sins (Mt 6:5–15).

First, Jesus sets the context for how his disciples are to pray. There are two models that they should avoid. One is "the hypocrites." These are the publically religious Jews that Jesus had very little patience with. They should have known better, but they prayed in order to be seen by other people. Their prayer was a show to impress others, but they forgot about the one person that they most needed to address. Jesus says that they got what they wanted from their prayer, but they certainly shouldn't expect an answer from God. They wanted to be seen by people, and they were. Today we generally don't face this kind of temptation from the culture at large, but there are still certain Christian circles and subcultures where praying out loud with others can become a performance. We're tempted to say things in a certain way to sound holy, smart, spiritual or whatever. If we forget that God is our main audience, then prayer drifts from being what it supposed to be. Jesus' warning is that when this happens, the greatest punishment is that we get what we wanted. We may be more highly viewed by others, but it isn't prayer toward God. The way to break this cycle is to go to God in secret and trust the goodness of God to give us what we need. This isn't to say that we should not pray with others. The early church, and Jesus himself with his disciples, shows us that prayer with others is powerful and honors God. Yet, when it's a show, God wants no part of it. Go to him because you want to go to him, not because you want to impress others.

The other model of prayer that Jesus warns against is that of the pagans. They, unlike the devout Jews, don't know who God truly is. They think they can manipulate God by their words. To them prayer is magic. If you say the right thing in the right way, perhaps you'll get the response you wanted. They ultimately don't know whom they are praying to. They misunderstand the character and nature of God himself, so that they think the success of their prayers depends on them. We are tempted in this direction in several ways, but one way is when we place too much emphasis on our own faith for getting answers to our prayers. Just to be clear at this point, I am not saying our faith doesn't matter. Jesus constantly talks about us having faith, and is constantly challenging his disciples to have more. He said that if we had faith the size of a mustard seed, we could move mountains. What I am saying is that the strength of faith is proportional to the faithfulness of the person or object we have faith in. We can place our faith in the wrong things, and then it doesn't matter how much faith we have, our faith is misplaced. For example, if you constantly loan someone money who never pays you back, and you keep doing it because you have faith that each time they will pay you, then it doesn't matter how much faith you have, you're putting your faith in an untrustworthy person. Putting it in another way, if a child were to ask his father to do something for him, the father would do it regardless of how much the child believes simply because he loves his child. The child has perfect faith because he or she knows the character and love of the father. It is the same with us and God. The reason we can and should have great faith in God is because he is infinitely worthy of our faith and trust. There is nothing he cannot do and his word is the standard by which words are judged true. When we are overly focused on our faith, we lose sight of the goodness of God and forget that our faith is based on his greatness not our ability to believe. We pray like pagans when we underestimate the goodness, power and love of our heavenly Father and think that we must compel an unwilling God to do what we want. Jesus assures us that God already knows and that he is eager to answer.

After clearing away two unhelpful approaches to prayer, Jesus lays out how his disciples should pray. It's clear that this isn't the only thing people should say while praying but rather a pattern and approach that should guide our prayer. He gives us a structure to fill out and an outline to follow.

Our Father in heaven

We should start our prayers by remembering whom we are addressing. These words express an intimacy that is staggering when compared to the rest of Scripture. Throughout Scripture God is approached with reverence and awe, often in real fear, and I'm sure if he appeared before us in all of his glory right now, we would fall on our faces as well. However, here Jesus invites us to call God our father, and a little further on in this same chapter Jesus emphasizes how God goes beyond even the best earthly fathers in his love, care, and ability to provide for his children. When you approach God in prayer, remember that you are coming to your father who holds his arms open wide to receive you. He wants to be with you. He desires to speak with you. He wants to show you his love. Jesus won our right to be children of God through his life, death, and resurrection. Go boldly to your heavenly Father, because Jesus has already prepared the way.

Hallowed be your name

Our first request is that God's name would be held in high regard. We saw earlier that a name represents a person. It is a person's reputation, and our desire is that God's reputation should be renowned. As our Father, we want people to honor him and to love him. We want people to think highly of him and see him for who he is. This is the kind of prayer that God delights to answer. What he has wanted from the beginning of time is that creation, and humanity as head of that creation, should have a clear vision of him and respond to him in loving adoration. When we pray that God's name would be hallowed, we pray for this. We pray that humanity along with all creation would join in worship to our God and king. If we use the

Lord's Prayer as our guide, this is a great place to offer our own adoration of God. We can worship him for his act of creation, for his attributes and perfections, for sending Jesus to die for us, for the fact that one day he will renew and remake the world, and for a whole host of other things. We can thank God for the blessings we experience in our own lives; for our health, families, jobs, and anything good that he has given to us. As we pray that more people would worship and praise God, we can begin by being one of them right in our prayer.

Your kingdom come, your will be done, on earth as it is in heaven.

After we have addressed God for who he is, asked that his name would be great and praised and thanked him for all of his greatness, now we ask that his kingdom would come. This request comes with an explanation that helps us understand what Jesus is talking about. Throughout the Old Testament, particularly in poetry like the Psalms or much of the prophetic writings, the authors speak in parallelism. They say one line and add a second line to it that builds upon and enhances the same sentiment. For instance, Psalm one verse one says, "Blessed is the man who does not walk in the council of the wicked or stand in the way of sinners or sit in the seat of mockers...." It essentially is saying the same thing in three different ways, giving us different angles to view the same image and in so doing it fills out the picture it is trying to paint of what a righteous person looks like. A righteous person doesn't walk, stand, or sit with evil people. In other words, a righteous person doesn't spend a lot of time in the company of the unrighteous. The parallelism helps drive the point home. Jesus is being a good Hebrew and doing the same thing here. He prays that God's kingdom would come, which means that God's will would be done on earth just as it is already done perfectly in heaven. Heaven is heaven because everything is done according to the way that God wants it done at every moment of every day in obedient joy, delight, and worship. For God's kingdom to come on earth would mean that God would rule perfectly on earth the way he already does in heaven. Everything God wants would happen all the time.

There are two ways to view what Jesus is asking us to pray, which I think are both equally true. The first is that God's kingdom would come in the ultimate sense, in the eschatological sense, where God is all in all. In praying this way, we are asking for God to intervene definitively to make the world the way it is supposed to be, to get rid of all sickness, famine, war, plague, death and sin, to bring about the vision that we see at the end of Revelation where the new Jerusalem descends and the dwelling place of God is finally with humanity forever. This is certainly what we are longing for when we pray this prayer. That day and that moment are, in a sense, the answer to every prayer. Once God's kingdom comes completely, all evil will be done away with and goodness and righteousness will flourish.

That is one way to pray for the kingdom to come, but there is another way as well, which gives immediacy to the words. This sense is that God's will would be done more and more in daily life and individual situations. There are tons of situations all around us every day where we know that God's will isn't being done. If people are being exploited, mistreated, unloved, lied to, neglected, or in any way sinned against, then God's will isn't being done and we should be praying for him to intervene and change things. In this way we are praying for signs of the kingdom to break through. It is as if at the end of a long cold winter we would pray for the trees to start budding and the flowers to sprout up. We want to see the signs that spring is on the way and that winter doesn't have the final word. In the same way we are praying for more justice, more love, more truth to break into the world that would show the kingdom is advancing. We long for God to make it permanent, and we pray that he would but we also pray that the signs of the kingdom would be more and more evident in our own lives and in the lives of people around us. In this simple request, God is giving us a mind-boggling power and task. He is charging us with looking at the world around us and taking its problems to him, so that they could be brought into alignment with his will, so that these broken places and situations could look more like heaven. Here we stand like priests between God and the world, taking the needs of the world to God and bringing the resources of heaven to bear on the world's problems. This part of the prayer is where we plead with God to act and fix the brokenness around us, broken marriages, addictions, unjust situations, people far from him and all the other needs we come across in our day-to-day lives. We have the joy and the privilege to be people who can take hopeless situations to our heavenly Father expecting him to act and bring goodness out of tragedy.

Give us today our daily bread.

The first half of Jesus' prayer is concerned about what God wants, and we would do well to pay attention to this point. If we are eager to see God answer prayers, we should pray the kind of prayers that God wants to answer, and what God wants more than anything is to be honored, worshipped and obeyed, not because he is selfish, but because the world works best when it is in right relation to him. When that happens, heaven comes to earth and everything is as it should be. The first half of the Lord's Prayer is focused on just that, but amazingly it doesn't stop there. Now the emphasis switches and our needs become the subject of the prayer. Just like Israel waiting for Manna in the desert, we are to ask each day for enough for that day. This is similar to the Psalm we already looked at which says, "In the morning, Lord, you hear my voice; in the morning I lay my requests before you and wait expectantly" (Ps 5:3). We would love to have an abundance, so that we know we'll be taken care of tomorrow and the day after, but we're instructed to simply pray for one day's needs at a time. I don't think this means we shouldn't save or plan for the future, but it does mean that we should have a simple daily trust in God to take care of us one day at a time. Just a little further on in the chapter Jesus tells us not to worry about tomorrow, because each day has enough worry for itself. This request in the prayer is the practical outworking of that teaching. Every day we have needs and every day we are invited to bring those needs, as ordinary and regular as they may seem, to God expecting him to meet them. Here is where we bring *all* of our needs to God, everything that is on our minds, everything we are worrying about, everywhere we have a lack, and need him to provide for us. We don't need to be anxious or afraid, because God knows what we need before we ask and he wants to take care of his children. We can trust that whatever we get will be enough and our Father will always provide for us.

And forgive us our debts, as we also have forgiven our debtors.

This first thing that we notice about this request is that it comes with what would seem to be a condition. Forgive us as we forgive. So, what does this mean? First, it isn't that we have to forgive first before God forgives us. The entire testimony of Scripture goes in the opposite direction. God's forgiveness is the basis for the forgiveness that we offer to others. The radical forgiveness we have received through the death of Jesus for our sins is the grounds for all other forgiveness. Paul says in Romans, "But God demonstrates his own love for us in this: While we were still sinners, Christ died for us" (Rom 5:8). God takes the initiative to forgive. It starts with him, and this is primary. So, once again, what does this mean?

Jesus tells a parable in Matthew 18 that helps put this request into proper perspective. In Matthew 18:21–35 Peter asks how often he should forgive someone who sins against him. Peter is looking for the cutoff point of forgiveness, but Jesus says in effect forgiveness is limitless. Jesus tells a story about a king who was settling accounts with his servants. One servant owed the king so much money it would have taken his whole lifetime to pay it back. The servant begged and pleaded for time to pay back the debt, but the king was merciful and forgave the entire debt so that the servant didn't have to pay him back. The servant left the king, and on his way, he saw another servant who owed him a fraction of the amount that he had owed the king, just a few months' wages. The first servant choked and intimidated the second servant demanding his money back, and the second servant begged for more time to come up with the money. The first servant, unlike the merciful king, didn't forgive him and had him thrown into prison until he got every last cent back. Some other servants of the king saw all this take place and took the news back to the king. The king called back the first servant, and in anger at the incomprehensibility of his lack of mercy of a small offense after he had been forgiven such a great debt, the king reinstates the debt and puts him in prison until he should pay it all. Jesus concludes the story saying, "This is how my heavenly Father will treat each of you unless you forgive your brother or sister from your heart" (Mt 18:35). The condition, if we want to call it that, of receiving ongoing forgiveness is offering ongoing forgiveness. It is as if God's grace and mercy are flowing through a pipe or a channel and unforgiveness blocks it. If we constantly offer the forgiveness we receive, then the channel will never stop flowing with grace and mercy. After we receive the initial forgiveness offered to us in Christ, we live in a relationship of constantly flowing grace, which this request in the Lord's Prayer recalls. This part of the prayer is where we confess our sins to God depending on the extravagant forgiveness that is on offer for us in Christ. We remember that whatever our sin, it is primarily against God that we commit it. We pray like David in the Psalms saying, "Have mercy on me, O God, according to your unfailing love; according to your great compassion blot out my transgressions. Wash away all my iniquity and cleanse me from my sin. For I know my transgressions, and my sin is always before me. Against you, you only, have I sinned and done what is evil in your sight" (Ps 51:1-4). We also ask that God would help us to forgive others just as we have been forgiven. Through this request we are keeping the channel of forgiveness open so that we can continue to receive mercy and offer it to others.

And lead us not into temptation, but deliver us from the evil one.

Jesus has so far taught us to praise God for who he is, pray for his will to be done in the world around us, ask for provision for our daily needs, and seek forgiveness even as we offer it. Now he instructs us to pray for protection. In *The Screwtape Letters* C.S. Lewis says we make two equal and opposite mistakes when it comes to demons, we either think about them too much or we don't think about them at all. It is possible to be so afraid of Satan that we forget that God is sovereign, infinitely more powerful and ultimately victorious. However, it is also possible to forget what Peter says about the evil one, which is "your enemy the devil prowls around like a roaring lion looking for someone to devour" (1 Pt 5:8). Either by church tradition or culture we're pulled in one of two directions, of either minimizing Satan or obsessing over him. However, Jesus strikes the proper balance by teaching us to ask God for the ability to avoid Satan's deceptions. He recognizes that our adversary is present, but Jesus tells us to go to our Father who can protect us. He protects us by helping us steer clear of temptation because the implication is that one of Satan's primary tactics is to bring us down through our own weakness and sin. Temptation isn't sin, but the best route to avoid sin is to avoid the temptation that leads to sin. Jesus teaches us to recognize our own fallibility and then ask God to keep us from it all. We've already prayed for forgiveness for our sins, but here with humility about our own weakness we ask God to spare us from testing that would lead to sin. We ask for patience for family members, coworkers, and friends. We ask for wisdom to clearly see the world around us because we fail and fall all too easily, and we need to be guided and helped. We'll be able to stand because God is powerful and able to make us stand (Rom 14:4).

ACTS

The Lord's Prayer offers a great pattern for how to pray, and we could do no better than to follow Jesus' advice. There is an acronym that doesn't mirror this prayer perfectly but does include its main elements. When I find myself wondering in my prayers I use the acronym ACTS, which stands for Adoration, Confession, Thanksgiving, and Supplication. In adoration, we praise God for who he is as our Father, king, creator, and so on. Having recognized the greatness of God, we confess our sins and how we fall short of his holiness. Next, we thank God for all the good we receive from him in our own lives. Personally, I always flow back and forth between adoration and thanksgiving because I don't think they can really be kept apart, but this is a place where we can count our blessings and thank God for what he has done for us personally. Finally, after having spent a good deal of time worshipping, thanking and confessing, just like in the

Lord's prayer, we bring our requests before God in supplication. Supplication means to ask for something humbly. Therefore, we ask God for the things we need knowing that we can't make him give anything, but we can ask in full confidence of his goodness as our heavenly Father. This acronym catches much of the heart of the Lord's Prayer and can be a helpful template to follow.

Perseverance in Prayer

Jesus had many lessons to teach his disciples about prayer, and he did it in many ways. As we saw he modeled a vibrant prayer life before them. He also gives them the content and pattern of how they should pray through the Lord's Prayer. He goes even further, however, giving them parables about perseverance in prayer. Let us consider two back to back. Immediately after the Lukan version of the Lord's Prayer, Jesus tells his disciples this,

> "Suppose you have a friend, and you go to him at midnight and say, 'Friend, lend me three loaves of bread; a friend of mine on a journey has come to me, and I have no food to offer him.' And suppose the one inside answers, 'Don't bother me. The door is already locked, and my children and I are in bed. I can't get up and give you anything.' I tell you, even though he will not get up and give you the bread because of friendship, yet because of your shameless audacity he will surely get up and give you as much as you need.

> "So I say to you: Ask and it will be given to you; seek and you will find; knock and the door will be opened to you. For everyone who asks receives; the one who seeks finds; and to the one who knocks, the door will be opened" (Lk 11:5–10).

Then he tells a parable in Luke 18, where it says,

> Then Jesus told his disciples a parable to show them
> that they should always pray and not give up. He said:
> "In a certain town there was a judge who neither
> feared God nor cared what people thought. And
> there was a widow in that town who kept coming to
> him with the plea, 'Grant me justice against my
> adversary.'

> "For some time he refused. But finally he said to
> himself, 'Even though I don't fear God or care what
> people think, yet because this widow keeps bothering
> me, I will see that she gets justice, so that she won't
> eventually come and attack me!'"

> And the Lord said, "Listen to what the unjust judge
> says. And will not God bring about justice for his
> chosen ones, who cry out to him day and night? Will
> he keep putting them off? I tell you, he will see that
> they get justice, and quickly. However, when the Son
> of Man comes, will he find faith on the earth"
> (Lk 18:1–8)?

In the first story a man comes to a friend at night asking
for food for his guests. The friend is understandably
annoyed but grants the request because of the sheer
boldness of it. In the second story a widow bothers an
unjust judge until she gets justice. In both cases, with the
sleeping friend and the unjust judge, it isn't because of
anything intrinsic to them the request is granted. It isn't
because they are great or even good that the appeal is
heard. It is because the person begging for help has the
nerve to ask, repeatedly if need be. Jesus assures us that
God isn't so reluctant and can be counted on to do good,
yet we should be like the shameless friend and the

persistent widow, asking until we get a response. We should keep coming to God over and over and over again until we get an answer. The answer may in fact be 'no', but Jesus teaches us that we don't annoy or bother God by continuing to ask in fact we honor him. When we are praying according to God's will, according to the things that we know he would want, we must keep praying until he responds. Jesus says that he will and we should take him at his word.

Praying the Scriptures

We can have no better teacher in how to pray than Jesus himself, but Scripture is full of prayers to study, practice and pray. Throughout the history of the church many have found it helpful to use these passages as the jumping off point for their own prayers. There are many passages you could choose and many ways to use them, but here is one way to use Scripture as a springboard into your own time of prayer followed by some suggestions for some portions of Scripture to use.

First the method: choose a relatively short passage of Scripture and read over it a few times. Read it slowly resting on the words that speak to you. Let the full sense of the words impact you. Gradually turn them into a prayer by asking God to reveal their full sense to you and by affirming them as true. As the words calm and focus your mind, enter into the presence of God praying however you're lead.

You can do this with the Lord's Prayer, but there are many others you can use as well. One of my favorite passages to pray in this way is Ephesians 3:16–19 where Paul says,

> I pray that out of his glorious riches he may strengthen you with power through his Spirit in your

inner being, so that Christ may dwell in your hearts through faith. And I pray that you, being rooted and established in love, may have power, together with all the Lord's holy people, to grasp how wide and long and high and deep is the love of Christ, and to know this love that surpasses knowledge—that you may be filled to the measure of all the fullness of God.

The image of the immeasurable love of God expressed in Christ is worth pondering and praying again and again. Romans 8 is full of excellent places to camp and take in the goodness of God that leads us into prayer, like when Paul says, "If God is for us, who can be against us? He who did not spare his own Son, but gave him up for us all—how will he not also, along with him, graciously give us all things" (Rom 8:31–32)? You could go to Jesus' prayer in John 17 to reflect on Jesus' passion for God's glory and for his disciples to make that glory known. Or why not do what generations and generations of believers have done and soak yourself in the Psalms? For centuries monks have prayed through the entire Psalter every week to learn the vast riches of the prayer book of the people of God. The Psalms contain some of the highest expressions of joy and praise along with the deepest outpourings of pain and despair. It is real and raw and it is all brought to God knowing that he can handle it and he alone can do something about it. You can go to many other places in Scripture for fuel for prayer, but if you let these texts master you, you'll have moved far into the deep things of prayer and will have certainly learned how to pray.

CHAPTER 5

The Power of Praying with Others

So far, we have looked at how to develop a personal prayer life. We've looked at the life of Jesus as our model for how to pray. We've talked about how to make time for prayer in our busy lives. We've examined the Lord's Prayer for a pattern and structure for our own prayers, plus how to use Scripture as a springboard into our own times of prayer. Now I want us to take some time to talk about praying with others. Without a personal prayer life our time of prayer with others has less effect, but without praying with others we miss the fullness that participating in the body of Christ in prayer brings. When we pray with other believers, and we see God provide answers to our prayers, it creates a unity and a strengthening of our faith that I believe God longs for. All throughout the book of Acts, we see the early church constantly at prayer together, and we see God answering in extraordinary ways. Therefore, I want to propose several ways that we can pray with others, which are not mutually exclusive. In fact, I would recommend engaging in each kind of prayer relationship as much as you can. These are basic and common-sense sort of suggestions, but most of us suffer from the fact that the basics seems so basic that we don't do them, and we are worse off for it. So, take this as a call to get back to the basics, realizing that our spiritual lives would be so much richer if we simply did what we knew we should do.

With your spouse

If you are married, one of the most important things you can do is pray with your spouse. There has been research to indicate that couples who pray together stay together. They are significantly less likely to get divorced than on average, and even compared to couples that attend church. So, praying together is an investment in both your spiritual life and your marriage.

Here are a couple of tips for starting and staying on track. First, start small. If you've never had a habit of praying together with your spouse, don't overcomplicate it by setting your sights too high. Take just a few moments to pray together when you have time. My wife and I typically pray together right before we go to bed. Sometimes just one of us prays, sometimes both, but we take a few moments right before bed to spend time with the Lord together. This leads to the second piece of advice, which is be consistent. If you can establish a very simple and short time of prayer together, and you do it consistently, it will quickly become a habit. You can always pray more or pray for longer, but the point is setting the bar low enough that you establish the habit. Once the habit is established, you can take it in whatever way you both desire but get the habit set up first. If you get knocked off course for any reason such as work, travel, kid's schedules, or the like, just start over again as soon as you can with a small but consistent time of prayer together. You'll grow closer to God and closer together through the process.

With a friend

If you are not married, or even if you are, you can benefit a great deal from finding a few close friends that you can share requests with and pray for. Jesus was always pulling Peter, James, and John aside with him in more intimate times of prayer. His disciples spent a great deal of time with him, but these three he allowed to have an inside track. They got to see and hear things that the others didn't. We should have at least a few people in our life that we give this kind of access and with whom we share areas where we need prayer. If this is a person you see on a regular basis that is great, but it can be a friend you connect with on the phone or online. You just need somebody, or a few, that you can share more freely with and know that they are supporting you in prayer and you are doing the same for them. You function, in a way, as one another's spiritual physicians checking in on the state of your hearts and spiritual health. It is good for both your spiritual and emotional health. All it takes to establish this kind of relationship is the two regular questions of 'how are you doing?' and 'how can I pray for you?' It is a privilege to be able to take other's requests before our heavenly Father, and it is exciting to see how God answers.

With a Group

The last thing you can do is find a small group of people that you can pray with on a regular basis. The book of Acts is full of the disciples coming together to pray and God immediately answering in amazing ways. There is something about this corporate dimension of prayer that delights our heavenly Father. When he sees his children coming together to ask for something for his glory and honor, he is that much more likely to respond. It is like the widow demanding justice from the unjust judge; only it isn't just her who comes day after day but all of her friends as well. An unjust judge can't ignore that many pleas for justice, and we can trust our heavenly Father to hear us all the more. We multiply our efforts when we pray with others and our faith is strengthened as we see the results. This past year I have been praying twice a week with the same few people, and I have been utterly astounded by what God has done as a result. On numerous occasions, we have been in the middle of praying for someone and that person texts to say that they're feeling better, or a problem has been solved, or they would like to get together, not knowing that we had been praying for them.

Perhaps you already have a small group or prayer group that you pray with, and if so, keep going. If not, then I would offer the same council in starting a prayer group as when starting to pray with your spouse. Start small and be consistent. If ultimately, you'd love to meet weekly, or even multiple times a week with others for prayer, start with a rhythm that is easy to keep. Maybe every other week or once a month would be better to start with than beginning by being overly ambitious and burning out. As people see the value, experience the results and encounter God, you can always get together more often. However, if you say you want to pray together every morning during the week, but only do it a few times, people will feel defeated and give up. Better to start small and add, then to start too big and feel crushed. After starting small comes staying consistent. If you have six people who consistently gather for prayer and half of you can't make it most of the time, keep the meeting. Occasionally you'll have to cancel. However, the more you cancel the more it begins to feel like it isn't really important. If it starts to feel like it isn't important, you'll cancel more often for more trivial reasons until it finally falls apart. Groups have life spans and all eventually come to an end in some form, but it's harder to resuscitate a dead group than it is to keep an irregular group going. The point isn't necessarily to keep the group going, the point is to pray together with others, but you'll experience much more benefit from a prayer group that lasts a while than constant prayer groups that always fizzle out quickly. You'll have a history with God together that strengthens you to keep asking, to keep knocking, and to keep seeking because you have all seen God answer, open and show you things again and again.

CHAPTER 6

Unanswered Prayer

Scripture makes some incredible promises when it comes to prayer, many on the lips of Jesus himself. Jesus promises, "Very truly I tell you, whoever believes in me will do the works I have been doing, and they will do even greater things than these, because I am going to the Father. And I will do whatever you ask in my name, so that the Father may be glorified in the Son. You may ask me for anything in my name, and I will do it" (Jn 14:12–14). He repeats twice that if we ask in his name, it will be given to us. He also says, "Truly I tell you, if you have faith as small as a mustard seed, you can say to this mountain, 'Move from here to there,' and it will move. Nothing will be impossible for you" (Mt 17:20).

So, how can we have such great promises and still not see answers to our prayers? Is it because of a lack of faith? In a lot of cases, yes, probably. Our lack of faith might be the reason we aren't seeing answers to our prayers, but let us remind ourselves again that our faith has to do with the faithfulness of the one we are believing. That is why Jesus chooses a mustard seed to emphasize that it is less about our faith and more about the greatness and goodness of God to act and do amazing things. I like the analogy that faith is a window through which we see the greatness of God. We could have a big window, a small, dirty, or distorted window to look through but God is still great and good on the other side. A clearer picture of God allows us to trust him more fully. So, when our view of God is small or distorted this absolutely effects how we pray and the answers, or lack thereof, that we receive. But what about when we do see God as big, as capable, and still don't get the answers we are looking for in prayer?

I would offer two initial points to consider. First, 'no' is an answer. Sometimes God does answer 'no,' and it isn't because we prayed incorrectly or asked for something wrong. He may in fact have a bigger purpose than what we grasp. As we saw earlier, Jesus prayed that if possible God would spare him the torment and shame of his death on the cross, but there was no other way. This was the heart of the very plan of God. There was no way around it. Jesus could only go through it and out the other side. If Jesus wouldn't have suffered and died, we would still be in our sins alienated from God. We also see something similar in the life of Paul. He says the following in 2 Corinthians, "Therefore, in order to keep me from becoming conceited, I was given a thorn in my flesh, a messenger of Satan, to torment me. Three times I pleaded with the Lord to take it away from me. But he said to me, 'My grace is sufficient for you, for my power is made perfect in weakness'" (2 Cor 12:7–9). We don't know what the "thorn" is, but we know that God used it in Paul's life to humble him and show his power through Paul's weakness. Both Paul and Jesus, through prayer, realized that God's 'no' had a purpose behind it, and both received 'no' as an answer.

The second point is that we don't know when God will

answer. This is especially true when we pray for healing from illness or disease. We may be praying diligently that God takes it away, but he doesn't. Godly people, who are being prayed for regularly, and who have great faith still suffer and die, and it wasn't because we were praying the wrong way or didn't believe enough. There is a mystery that the people of God have experienced from the fall of man onward, which is summed up in the question "How long, O Lord?" We know that God is good and we know that he is powerful, so when is he going to do something? When will he act? How long before all disease, sickness, suffering and death are done away with? This question has no simple answer. Sometimes we receive a foretaste of the age to come. We get a taste of the heavenly rule of God through a healing whether big or small. We see those signs of the kingdom that we spoke about earlier, like flowers poking through the snow to announce that spring will arrive soon. We can pray these kind of prayers without adding a tentative "if it's your will," because we know it is God's will. We know that God's will is to heal, to do justice, and to make earth like heaven. We don't have to soften these prayers, because God will ultimately answer them. Death and sin are an intrusion on God's good creation, and his firm desire is to do away with everything that spoils the world that he made. One day God will wipe away every tear and will make all things right, and in that day all prayers for healing, justice, and the coming of the rule of God will get their answer. Therefore, pray boldly knowing that all of your prayers according to his will already have their "yes" in Christ.

Taking it Deeper

———————

I don't pretend to give the definitive word on prayer. There are many who can teach you much about how to pray. Here are a few classic books on prayer that if read and applied will continue to deepen your prayer life. These authors have spent time in the presence of God, and we should listen to what they have to say. So, in no particular order here are several books that can take you deeper in prayer:

The Practice of the Presence of God, by Brother Lawrence

Brother Lawrence learned and practiced a simple style of prayer that kept him in God's presence all day long. He felt closer to God working in the kitchen of his monastery than he did during spiritual retreats or fixed times of prayer, because he knew God was always with him listening and talking. This book will teach you that praying at all times and in all sorts of ways is possible.

With Christ in the School of Prayer, by Andrew Murray

Andrew Murray is like a more experienced student taking you under his wing in Jesus' school of prayer. He has learned many lessons and he's eager to help you learn them too. This book is written with thirty-one chapters, which makes it great devotional reading for a month. I come back to it again and again, when I need reminded that God promises to answer and will answer any prayer made in Christ's name.

Experiencing the Depths of Jesus Christ, by Jeanne Guyon

Jean Guyon wrote this book to explain her method of prayer to people who were begging for her to teach them as well. She will teach you how to pray the Scriptures and seek Christ who is nearer to you than you can possibly imagine. Her burden is that those who consider themselves weak and simple would learn that they could have a deep and rich communion with the God of the universe.

Prayer: Finding the Heart's True Home, by Richard Foster

Richard Foster knows prayer, and he helps explain the rich variety of communication with God that is on offer for all of us. He walks you through the what and the how of prayer giving a lot of practical advice along the way. He wants you to know that you can have more and that your experience of prayer can be richer, more powerful, and more fulfilling than you ever thought possible.

Power through Prayer, by E.M. Bounds

E.M. Bounds gives you chapter after chapter of encouragement to pray. If you need some encouragement to start praying, look no farther than E.M. Bounds. He wants you to know that you have infinite power at your disposal, if you will but pray.

The Kneeling Christian, by An Unknown Christian

Similar to E.M. Bounds An Unknown Christian will give you encouragement and will encourage you to pray. This book is full of examples of what a vibrant prayer life looks like. One of my favorite chapters is where he answers the question of how much we should pray. He gives example after example of all sorts of people, businessmen, missionaries, and others, who decided that they needed to pray more and once they did, they saw God do amazing things. After that chapter, you'll be ready to do the same.

ABOUT THE AUTHOR

Ryan Bennett was born and raised in Ohio and attended the Ohio State University and Gordon-Conwell Theological Seminary where he received a Master of Divinity and a Master of Theology in Biblical Theology. He is a missionary church-planter with World Team. He and his wife Erin live with their son in Paris, France.

95837308R00035

Made in the USA
Columbia, SC
18 May 2018